Tons of Trucks!

DUMP TRUCKS

By Martin Harasymiw

Gareth Stevens
PUBLISHING

Please visit our website, www.garethstevens.com. For a free color catalog of all our high-quality books, call toll free 1-800-542-2595 or fax 1-877-542-2596.

Library of Congress Cataloging-in-Publication Data
Names: Harasymiw, Martin, 1978- author.
Title: Dump trucks / Martin Harasymiw.
Description: New York : Gareth Stevens Publishing, 2022. | Includes index.
Identifiers: LCCN 2020024428 (print) | LCCN 2020024429 (ebook) | ISBN 9781538262757 (library binding) | ISBN 9781538262733 (paperback) | ISBN 9781538262740 (set) | ISBN 9781538262764 (ebook)
Subjects: LCSH: Dump trucks–Juvenile literature.
Classification: LCC TL230.15 .H3679 2022 (print) | LCC TL230.15 (ebook) | DDC 629.225–dc23
LC record available at https://lccn.loc.gov/2020024428
LC ebook record available at https://lccn.loc.gov/2020024429

First Edition

Published in 2022 by
Gareth Stevens Publishing
111 East 14th Street, Suite 349
New York, NY 10003

Editor: Therese Shea
Designer: Deanna Paternostro

Photo credits: Cover, p. 1 Faraways/Shutterstock.com; p. 5 CSA Images/CSA Images/Getty Images; p. 7 Martin Diebel/Getty Images; pp. 9, 24 (load) Westend61/Getty Images; p. 11 Natasha-Aleksandra/iStock/Getty Images Plus/Getty Images; p. 13 Juan Silva/DigitalVision/Getty Images; pp. 15, 24 (cab) Douglas Sacha/Moment Open/Getty Images; p. 17 Juan Jose Napuri/iStock/Getty Images Plus/Getty Images; p. 19 tfoxfoto/iStock/Getty Images Plus/Getty Images; p. 21 WIN-Initiative/Stone/Getty Images; p. 23 Kamonrat Meunklad/EyeEm/EyeEm/Getty Images.

Printed in the United States of America

CPSIA compliance information: Batch #CSGS22: For further information contact Gareth Stevens, New York, New York at 1-800-542-2595.

Contents

This is my toy truck.
It's a dump truck!

This is a real
dump truck.
It's big!

Dump trucks carry loads.

Dump trucks carry dirt and rocks. They carry leaves and snow too.

The load goes
in the bed.

bed

The driver sits
in the cab.
The truck moves
the load.

cab

The bed tips up.
The load falls out.

Dump trucks are called tipper trucks!

This is a super dump!
It carries very big loads.

Dump trucks help!

Words to Know

cab

load

Index